SCHOLAST Follow-the-Directi

EASY ORIGAMI

Adorable Folded Paper Projects With Super-Easy Directions and Rebus Support That Build Beginning Reading Skills

BY DEBORAH SCHECTER

New York • Toronto • London • Auckland • Sydney
Mexico City • New Delhi • Hong Kong • Buenos Aires

Teaching *Resources*

For my forever friends—
Lynn, Leah, and Elise

Cover design by Jason Robinson
Interior design by Solas
Interior illustrations by Kate Flanagan

ISBN-13: 978-0-545-11081-5
ISBN-10: 0-545-11081-5

Text © 2009 by Deborah Schecter
Illustrations ® 2009 by Scholastic
Published by Scholastic Inc. All rights reserved. Printed in the U.S.A.

1 2 3 4 5 6 7 8 9 10   40   17 16 15 14 13 12 11 10 09

Contents

Origami Activities

Introduction

Welcome to *Follow-the-Directions Art: Easy Origami*, a collection of simple, folded paper projects just right for young learners. Children will be amazed that they can transform a sheet of paper into kites, whales, butterflies, farm animals, party hats, and other fun shapes. Easy-to-read directions with rebus pictures give children the support they need to complete each project independently and successfully. In addition to helping children build fine motor skills, these tactile projects include other learning benefits. Children will practice reading and following directions, count, identify shapes and colors, and develop directionality and spatial sense. (See Connections to the Standards, page 7, to see how the activities correlate to early childhood standards in language arts, math, and art.)

Once children have mastered a favorite project, you may find your classroom teeming with fun and friendly fish, mice, and puppy dogs! You can further enhance the learning experience with the following classroom connections. Examples follow.

❖ Complement holiday, seasonal, and special events as well as favorite themes such as All About Me, animals, plants, transportation, the farm, and life cycles.

❖ Enrich dramatic play and oral language activities using projects such as Pink Piggy Puppet (page 44), Chatty Cow Puppet (page 48), Big Bird Mask (page 58), Perfect Party Hat (page 60), and Cool Crown (page 62).

❖ Embellish bulletin boards, storage containers, or folders with the crafts and use them as springboards for cards, poems, stories, or nonfiction reports.

You'll find other ideas for using the projects in the Teaching Notes (pages 8–13).

Preparing for the Activities

❖ Packs of origami paper are not necessary for completing the folded paper projects in this book. Although it's helpful to use thin paper, which creases well and folds flat, you can use recycled copy paper or construction paper because each project consists of only a few basic folds. Paper that is colored on one side and white on the other, such as wrapping paper, is recommended for some projects.

❖ To make most of the projects, children will need just a large square of paper. Prepare 8 ½-inch or 9-inch squares of paper in different colors. Or make bigger squares using larger sheets of paper. If you have access to a paper cutter, you can precut an ample supply. (For a few of the projects—the Big Bird Mask (page 58), Perfect Party Hat (page 60), and Cool Crown (page 62)—you'll need 20-inch paper squares. Wrapping paper and craft paper work well for these projects.)

Teaching Tip
Although folding and cutting a rectangular sheet of paper may be an easy way to create a square, this can leave a crease that interferes with the origami folds. For best results, measure and cut the squares. Or use one of the square templates provided on page 64 and the inside back cover of this book. (You might create tagboard templates and set up a paper-cutting center where children can trace and cut out squares to help stock the class supply.)

Penguin Pal

1. **Fold** a white paper diamond in half from side to side. Then **unfold.**

2. **Fold** in the two sides so they meet at the middle.

3. **Fold** down the thin top corner. This is the penguin's head.

4. **Turn** the paper over. **Fold** up the wide bottom corner.

5. **Fold** back on the middle crease.

6. **Pull** up on the beak. Then **press** the head flat.

7. **Fold** back the flap on each side **to make** flippers.

8. **Color** your penguin. **Draw** a face.

Make your penguin walk and waddle!

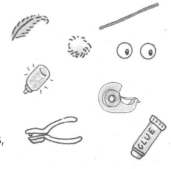

❖ Provide crayons and markers so that children can add personal touches to their projects. Also have on hand an assortment of craft and collage materials, such as colorful paper scraps, wiggle eyes, sequins, glitter glue, pompoms, craft feathers, paper hole reinforcements, yarn, and pipe cleaners. You'll also need tools and supplies, such as glue sticks, tape, hole punches, and left-hand and right-hand safety scissors.

❖ If possible, make the origami craft ahead of time to become familiar with the steps involved and to anticipate problems children may encounter, as well as to identify teaching opportunities. See Making Math Connections, page 6, for some suggestions.

❖ Each project includes an easy-to-make mini-poster that shows the step-by-step directions. To assemble the mini-posters, glue or tape the first page to the top of the second page, as indicated. Enlarge the pages, if desired. (The project directions on pages 18–22 each consist of a single page and require no assembly.)

❖ Highlight any color words in the directions in the corresponding color. You might also color some of the picture clues to match, for example, the color of the paper children will be using.

❖ These activities work well at learning centers. Place the materials and tools needed for the project at a center. Post a copy of the directions so that one or two students at a time can easily read them. You might also display a sample set of materials next to the directions so that children can check to see if they have what they need to complete the project.

Introducing the Activities

❖ Before children begin, find out what they know about origami. Explain that origami is a Japanese word that means "paper folding." Using this ancient art technique, they'll be able to transform a single sheet of paper into an amazing creation—such as a sailboat, space shuttle, puppy, or penguin.

❖ Discuss the importance of reading and following directions. Ask questions, such as "Why is it important to follow the steps in order?" and "What might happen if you skip a step?" Point out the numerals at the beginning of each step to reinforce sequential order.

❖ Review with children the materials and tools needed for an activity (paper, scissors, crayons, glue sticks, and so on).

❖ Read each step and check that children understand what to do. Review any text that may be unfamiliar.

Teaching Tip

To help children understand why the sequence in a set of directions is important, try this: Cut the step-by-step directions for a project into strips. Then scramble the strips and place in a pocket chart. Ask children if they think the directions make sense. Then challenge children to put the steps in the correct order.

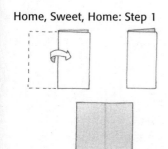
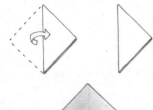
❖ Help children focus on the key action words (set in boldface type), such as *fold, unfold, turn, cut, draw, glue,* and *tape.*

❖ Review positional words and phrases such as *middle, top, bottom, up, down, over,* and *from side to side,* as well as the names of geometric shapes and concepts (*square, diamond, triangle, rectangle,* and *half*).

❖ Point out clues children can use to help them decode the text (rebus-style pictures above certain words, numerals, highlighted color words, directional arrows, and illustrations that show how the project looks at each stage). Children can use these elements as a guide to check that they are following the directions correctly.

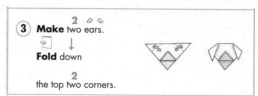

❖ Model for children how to make a project, showing them how it looks after completing each step. In particular, guide them to notice how to position the paper in each step. For example, in step 1 of each project, the directions use the terms *square* or *diamond* and include corresponding diagrams to indicate the starting position of the paper. (See Making Math Connections, below, for more.) Also point out that many of the diagrams show a light and darker side to the paper; this has been done to ensure that each side of the paper shows up clearly in the illustrations.

Making Math Connections

Origami offers many opportunities for helping children explore math skills, concepts, and vocabulary that involve spatial reasoning, geometry, symmetry, and simple fractions. Examples follow.

IDENTIFYING SHAPES

Give each child a paper square, rectangle, and triangle. Discuss the attributes of each shape. Then tell children to turn the square so that one corner points up and one points down. Explain that when a square is turned like this, it is sometimes called a *diamond*. Guide children to notice and compare the position of the paper in steps 1 of Home, Sweet, Home (page 18) and Simple Sailboat (page 21), for example. Also point out the corresponding positions of the pictures above the words *square* and *diamond* in the directions for each of these steps. Tell children that these pictures show how they should place the paper in that step.

Repeat this process with the triangle cutout, having children turn the triangle first sideways, and then upside down. Then have them compare the position of the folded paper triangle in steps 1 of Simple Sailboat (page 21) and Springtime Tulip (page 30). Point out the corresponding positions of the triangle pictures above the word *triangle* in the directions. Explain that these pictures also show how to place the folded paper triangle.

Tips for Success

❖ Have children work on a hard, flat surface.

❖ Let children practice folding squares of scrap paper, first lining up edges and corners, and then using their fingernails or a ruler to make sharp creases, as well as unfolding the paper.

❖ In the Teaching Notes (pages 8–15), the simplest projects are indicated with a star. Leveling tips for some of the projects and ideas for using the projects to extend learning appear in this section as well.

❖ If children are doing the activity with their own copy of the directions, suggest that they check off each step as they complete it.

EXPLORING SYMMETRY

Have children fold two paper squares in half—one from side to side and the other from corner to corner—and then unfold. Guide them to notice that they have created two rectangles and two triangles. Point out that the shapes are symmetrical—exactly the same on each side of the middle fold.

As children complete each step of a project, encourage them to describe and compare and contrast the different shapes that take form. When they have finished, have them unfold the craft and see how many different shapes they can identify and count in the creased paper.

Connections to the Standards

The lessons and activities in this book support the PreK–1 language arts, math and art standards as outlined by Mid-continent Research for Education and Learning (McRel), a nationally recognized, nonprofit organization that collects and synthesizes national and state K–12 curriculum standards.

Reading

• Understands how print is organized and read

• Uses mental images based on pictures and print to aid in comprehension of text

• Uses phonetic and structural analysis to decode unknown words

• Understands level-appropriate sight words and vocabulary

• Uses reading skills and strategies to understand and interpret informational texts such as written directions and procedures

Math

• Understands that numerals are symbols used to represent quantities or attributes of real-world objects

• Counts by ones to ten or higher

• Counts objects

• Knows the written numerals 0–9

• Understands that a whole object can be separated into parts

• Knows basic geometric language for naming shapes (for example, circle, triangle, square, rectangle)

• Understands the common language used to describe position and location (for example, "up," "down," "below," "above," "beside")

Visual Arts

• Experiments with a variety of colors, textures, and shapes

• Uses a variety of basic art materials to create works of art

• Knows the names of basic colors

Source: Kendall, J. S. & Marzano, R. J. (2004). *Content knowledge: A compendium of standards and benchmarks for K–12 education.* Aurora, CO: Mid-continent Research for Education and Learning. Online database: http://www.mcrel.org/standards-benchmarks/

Teaching Notes

Home, Sweet, Home ◈ (page 18)

Materials (for each child): one paper square, crayons or markers.

Variation: To make an apartment building, invite children to glue or tape additional paper squares to the bottom of their houses and decorate.

Extending the Activity: Children might glue their houses to a large sheet of paper, add several Wintertime Trees (page 22) to the scene, and then write or dictate a few sentences about their picture. Or, you might use children's houses as the basis for a neighborhood or community bulletin-board display.

Valentine Mailer ◈ (page 19)

Materials: heart template (page 16), scissors, pink or red paper. For each child: crayons, craft and collage materials, such as paper doilies and glitter glue; one sticker.

Tip: In advance, use the heart template to trace and cut out a class supply of pink or red paper hearts.

Extending the Activity: Let children "send" valentines to each other on February 14th. Secretly give each child the name of a classmate to make a valentine for so that each child will receive one. (If you have an odd number of students, make the extra one yourself.) Help children write their Valentine's name on the outside of the mailer and then deposit it in a class mailbox for distribution on the special day. (To make a "mailbox," see Perfect Party Hat Variation, page 15.)

Super Space Shuttle ◈ (page 20)

Materials (for each child): one paper square, crayons or markers.

Extending the Activity: Give each child a sheet of dark blue or black construction paper. Have children glue their shuttles to the paper, paint fiery orange and red rocket fuel coming out of the bottom, and then use glitter glue to create a starry outer space scene. Invite children to write or dictate stories about their space shuttle's trip.

Simple Sailboat ◈ (page 21)

Materials (for each child): one paper square, crayons or markers.

Tip: In steps 1 and 2 of this project, children will create the same basic form they will use for many of the projects that follow.

Extending the Activity: Let children "float" their boats! In advance, fold large, uncoated paper plates in half. Then cut a scalloped slit through the fold, from rim to rim. Make one for each child. Invite children to paint their "seas." When the paint is dry, children slip their boat into the slit and then gently tip the plate to make their boats bob up and down in the waves.

Wintertime Tree ◇ (page 22)

Materials (for each child): one green paper square, white glitter glue.

Extending the Activity: To make festive holiday trees, have children make colored paper dots using a hole punch and scrap paper, then glue the dot "ornaments" to their trees. (Or use self-adhesive colored dots.) Children can also make holiday cards for their friends and families by gluing their trees to folded sheets of construction paper and writing a greeting inside.

All About Me ◇ (page 24)

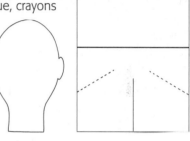

Materials: head and shirt templates (pages 16–17), scissors, construction paper in skin tones, colored copy paper. For each child: scissors, glue stick, craft glue, crayons or markers, three ½- to ¾-inch buttons (or same-size self-adhesive colored dots).

Tips: (1) In advance, trace the head pattern onto sheets of construction paper in different skin tones, then cut them out. (2) Make and cut out copies of the shirt template.

Extending the Activity: Try this project at the start of the school year to help children get to know their classmates. On a speech-bubble cutout, write "My name is _____. I like to _____." Photocopy a class supply and give one to each child. Invite children to fill in the blanks. Then create a bulletin-board display at children's eye level. Pin up each child's project positioning the speech bubble near his or her face. Let children take turns reading their speech bubble, elaborating on what they wrote if desired.

High-Flying Kite ◇ (page 26)

Materials (for each child): one paper square, 6- to 8-inch length of yarn (or longer depending on the size of the paper squares used), craft glue, painted bow-tie pasta (see Tips, below), tempera paints in different colors, paint brushes, crayons, markers, craft materials, such as glitter glue and self-adhesive colored dots.

Tips: (1) You might have children tape the yarn to the back of the kite instead of using glue. (2) Have children paint the bow-tie pasta ahead of time and let the paint dry completely before gluing to the yarn kite tail. (3) Instead of using bow ties, give children short pieces of colorful yarn or ribbon to tie to the kite tail.

Extending the Activity: Use the kites to give children practice with positional words and phrases. Direct children to "fly" their kites in different ways. Examples might include: "Fly your kite . . *up in the sky; in front of* you; *next to* you; *from left to right*."

Ice Cream Cone◇ (page 28)

Materials (for each child): two same-size paper squares, (in "ice-cream" colors, such as pink, brown, and light green), glue stick, glitter glue, craft glue, colored paper dots (children can make these using a hole punch and scrap paper), and other craft and collage materials.

Extending the Activity: Use the ice cream cones for a writing activity. Have children skip step 6 in which they add toppings to their cones. On the ice cream scoop, help them write the ice cream flavor, and on the cone, two or three words that describe ice cream (for example, *cold, creamy, smooth, sweet*). Invite children to roam the room and share their cones with classmates.

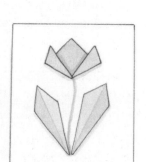

Springtime Tulip (page 30)

Materials (for each child): one paper square, any color except green (for the flower) and two green paper squares (for the leaves), one sheet of 9- by 12-inch (or larger) construction paper, glue stick.

Extending the Activity: Invite children to write poems that welcome or celebrate spring and display them on a bulletin board. Surround the poems with children's colorful tulips.

Pretty Picture Frame (page 32)

Materials (for each child): one paper square, photo or picture, glue stick, crayons, scrap paper, glitter glue, and other craft and collage materials.

Tips: (1) In step 4, point out to children that they should return the paper square to the diamond position. (2) To fit a bigger picture inside the frame, children can fold back the four triangles so they extend beyond the sides. The frame can also be turned as shown.

Extending the Activity: Instead of putting pictures inside the frames, use them to showcase samples of children's stories or poems. Display the frames where children can read each other's work.

Friendly Fish (page 34)

Materials (for each child): one paper square, crayons, glitter glue, sequins and other craft and collage materials.

Variation: To make a fish with a tail that points up, children can stop after step 5 and then add decorative details.

Extending the Activity: Help children research and write facts about fish on the back of their projects. Then make several "School of Fishy Facts" mobiles by taping different lengths of yarn to several fish and tying the other ends to coat hangers.

Wonderful Whale (page 36)

Materials (for each child): one paper square, scissors, crayons, glue stick, short lengths of white or blue narrow, curly ribbon.

Tip: In step 6, assist children who need help cutting the slit in the whale's tail.

Extending the Activity: Give each child a sheet of blue construction paper. To suggest ocean waves, help children cut scallops along the straight edge (or do this in advance). Next, children tape or glue the bottom of their whales to the scalloped edge of the paper, and then turn the paper over. Encourage children to write a few words or a sentence about their whale on their blue paper ocean.

Munching Mouse (page 38)

Materials (for each child): one paper square (use sturdy construction paper), crayons or markers, scrap paper, scissors, glue stick, yarn, one smaller, yellow paper square and a hole punch (for the cheese).

Tips: (1) In step 5, have children draw the face of the mouse on the thin corner of the paper. (2) In step 6, children may need help when they overlap and tape the sides of the paper together.

Extending the Activity: Let children use their mice during shared reading. Write the nursery rhyme "Hickory, Dickory, Dock" on chart paper. Read the rhyme once, and then reread it, inviting children to act out the rhyme by making the mouse run up and down the clock (their outstretched arms).

Cute Kitty Cat (page 40)

Materials (for each child): one paper square, two wiggle eyes, glue stick, craft glue, pompom, crayons or makers.

Variation: Instead of gluing the cat's head to its body, children can give their kitty cats movable heads! Punch a hole at the bottom of the head and at the top of the body. Then use a brad to fasten the two parts together.

Extending the Activity: Let children use the kitty-cat crafts and this fill-in poem to solve simple subtraction problems. Write each line of the poem on a separate sentence strip and place in a pocket chart. Then write the numerals 0 to 5 on separate cards and place at the bottom of the

> 5 little kitty cats
> sitting on a fence,
> _____ jumped off
> and then _____ were left!

chart. Place five kitty cats across the top. Read aloud the poem and invite children to join in as you reread it. Then place a numeral card, for example, "2," over the blank in line 3. Invite a volunteer to move the corresponding number of cats to the pocket for that line. Let another volunteer solve the problem by placing the correct numeral card and number of cats in the pocket for line 4.

Perky Puppy Dog (page 42)

Materials (for each child): one paper square, crayons or markers, pink scrap paper, scissors.

Variation: To make puppy masks that children can wear, use 20- by 20-inch paper squares (newsprint or wrapping paper work well) for the puppy's head and skip steps 5–7. Help children cut eyeholes. Then punch a hole in each side and tie on lengths of string for tying around children's heads.

Extending the Activity: What do children's puppy dogs have to say? Invite children to fill in speech-bubble cutouts for their dogs. Display children's puppy dogs on a bulletin board, positioning the speech bubbles near the dogs' mouths. Help children build reading fluency by encouraging them to read with expression.

Pink Piggy Puppet (page 44)

Materials (for each child): one pink paper square, scissors, two wiggle eyes, craft glue, two reinforcement labels, craft stick, tape.

Extending the Activity: Share with children the story of the "Three Little Pigs," such as the engaging version by James Marshall (Penguin, 1996). After discussing the story, divide the class into groups of three and invite children to use their puppets in a retelling. Children may also enjoy making up short skits that chronicle the further adventures of the three little pigs. Invite groups to use their puppets to perform their skits for the rest of the class.

Little Red Pecking Hen (page 46)

Materials (for each child): one red paper square, glue stick, crayons or markers, two craft feathers.

Extending the Activity: Give each child a few kernels of unpopped popcorn. Tell children to gently press down on the hen's tail to see their feathered friend peck and "eat" the corn. Follow up by sharing the classic story of the Little Red Hen (the version by Paul Galdone, originally published by Clarion Books in 1973, is an excellent rendition of this old favorite). Once children have become familiar with the story, invite them to work in small groups to do an oral retelling. They can use their Little Red Pecking Hens and other origami farm animals to portray the characters. (For directions on making a mouse, a cat, and a dog, see pages 38–43.)

Chatty Cow Puppet (page 48)

Materials (for each child): one 9- to 11-inch paper square, glue stick, two paper reinforcement labels, scrap paper (pink and other colors), scissors.

Tips: (1) When drawing the face on their cow, children should make sure to position the folded paper so the open edges are in the back. (2) To use their puppets, have children insert the four fingers of one hand in the top opening at the back, and their thumb in the bottom opening. Children then open and close their hand to make their cow "talk." Invite children to pair up and invent conversations between their cows!

Variation: To make a lamb or sheep instead of a cow, provide children with cotton balls (wool) to glue between the ears.

Extending the Activity: For a phonics connection, write words that contain the vowel diphthong *ow* on index cards (*chow, cow, how, now, plow, pow, wow*). On separate cards, write words that contain the same spelling pattern but are pronounced using the long-*o* sound (*blow, crow, grow, know, slow, snow*). Review both sets of words with children. Then mix up the cards and show children one card at a time. Invite volunteers to use their puppets and best cow voices to read each word and use it in a sentence.

Big Red Barn (page 50)

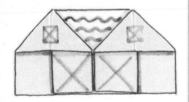

Materials (for each child): one red paper square, crayons or markers.

Tip: Children may need help opening the folded corners in step 6.

Extending the Activity: Instead of drawing animals inside their barns, children can open the doors and write or dictate a story inside. Topics might include different animals that live in the barn, what the animals talk about at night when the doors are closed, or favorite places on a farm.

Slither-and-Slide Snake (page 52)

Materials (for each child): one lightweight paper square, crayons or markers, tape.

Tips: (1) Thin wrapping paper that is colored on one side and white on the other works best for this project. Or give children squares of white copy paper and have them color or decorate one side. (2) Have children make folds that are about one inch deep. (3) In step 7, it doesn't matter how many folds children make in their snakes. However, it is important that they make sharp creases.

Extending the Activity: Use the snakes to introduce onomatopoeia—words that mimic the sound they describe. Ask, "What sound does a snake make?" (*hiss*). Explain that some words, like *hiss*, sound like their meanings. Invite children to make their snakes slither and slide, and hiss, exaggerating and drawing out the word as they say it. Then brainstorm with children other animal-sound words that sound like what they mean, such as *meow, moo, buzz,* and *squeak.*

Fluttering Butterfly (page 54)

Materials (for each child): one 8-inch and one 10-inch paper square (use lightweight paper such as wrapping paper in different colors or patterns), pipe cleaner.

Tips: (1) You can use paper squares that are larger than the sizes suggested; just be sure to make one square two inches larger than the other. (2) When pleating the paper, remind children to make sharp creases along the entire length of each fold. (3) Before fastening together the two sets of wings with the pipe cleaner, have children line up the two sheets of pleated paper in the middle so that the wings are evenly spaced on each side. (4) To simplify the project, have children make only one set of wings.

Extending the Activity: To make butterflies that really flutter and fly, tie a thin piece of string around the pipe cleaner antennae. Then go outdoors and invite children to hold the string and make their butterflies fly in different ways. Brainstorm with children vivid action words that can be used to describe how their butterflies move, such as *zip, zoom, loop, swoop, spin, dip,* and *dive.* Back inside, invite children to use some of these words to write or dictate a poem about their butterfly.

Penguin Pal (page 56)

Materials (for each child): one white paper square, crayons or markers.

Extending the Activity: To make their penguins waddle, children can gently pull on the flippers and rock the animal from side to side as they move it forward. Then help children do research to learn other ways penguins get around. For example, they toboggan on their bellies to move quickly over ice and snow, hop from rock to rock, dive into the water and swim to find food, and then hop back onto land.

Big Bird Mask (page 58)

Materials (for each child): one 20- by 20-inch paper square, scissors, hole punch, two 12-inch lengths of string, crayons or makers, glue, scrap paper, craft feathers and other collage materials.

Tips: (1) In step 5, have children fold down the thin corner so it is positioned just below the tip of the wide corner. (2) To give the beak more shape, show children how to fold the mask back along the middle crease, unfold, and then lift up the beak again. (3) In step 9, give children crayons, scrap paper, craft feathers, sequins, and other craft materials for decorating their masks.

Extending the Activity: Use the masks to help build oral language skills. Suggest that children work in small groups to make up skits starring bird characters, then wear their masks when performing the skits for classmates.

Perfect Party Hat (page 60)

Materials (for each child): one 20- by 20-inch paper square, crayons or markers, glue, yarn, scrap paper, craft feathers, and other collage materials.

Variations: (1) To make a duck or bird hat, children can leave one flap down to suggest a beak. (2) To turn the hat into a hanging wall pocket or mailbox, leave one flap down. Then turn the project upside down and tack the flap to a bulletin board.

Extending the Activity: Use the party hats to motivate, reinforce, and reward positive behavior. Label a sentence strip with a weekly class behavior goal, such as cleaning up promptly or lining up quietly. Display it with a sample party hat alongside. Tell children that they will have a party if the class earns ten feathers to decorate the hat by the end of the week. At the end of each day, review with children whether or not they earned any feathers and attach to the hat accordingly. At the end of the week, count the feathers to see if the class met its goal. If so, invite children to celebrate! Have them don their party hats and give them a small reward such as a fun-shaped eraser or other small treat.

Cool Crown (page 62)

Materials (for each child): four 8-inch paper squares in contrasting colors, tape, crayons or markers, pompoms, glitter glue, stickers, plastic gems, and other collage materials.

Tip: Children may need help in step 5, when they insert the folded corners inside one another.

Extending the Activity: Invite children to wear their crowns to act out favorite nursery rhymes, such as "The Queen of Hearts" and "Sing a Song of Sixpence" or stories that they make up. And to make birthday celebrations extra special, let the birthday child wear his or her crown while classmates put on their Perfect Party Hats (page 60).

Valentine Mailer
Heart Template

(See page 8.)

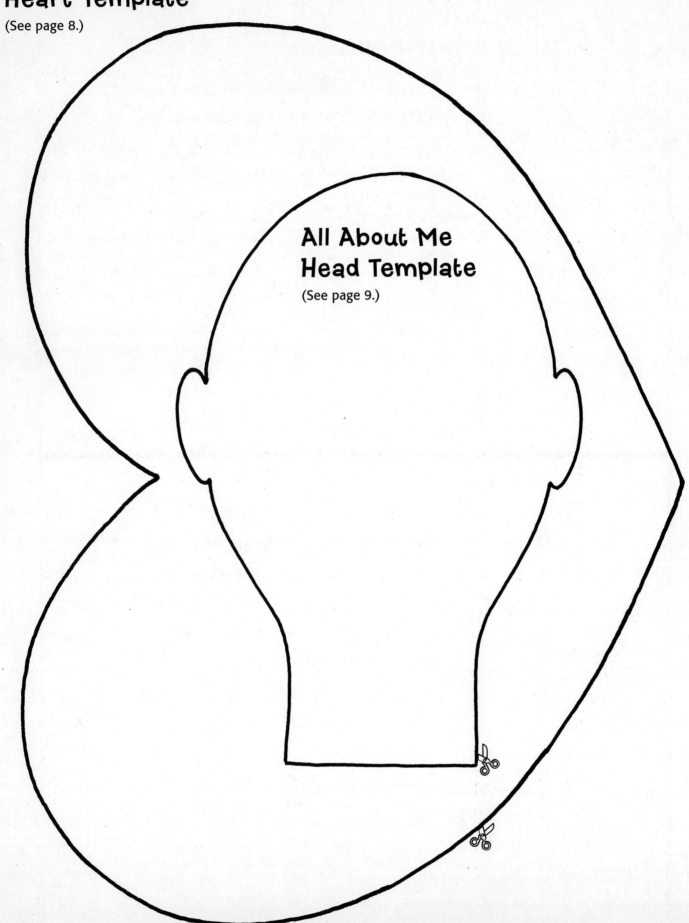

All About Me
Head Template

(See page 9.)

All About Me Shirt Template (See page 9.)

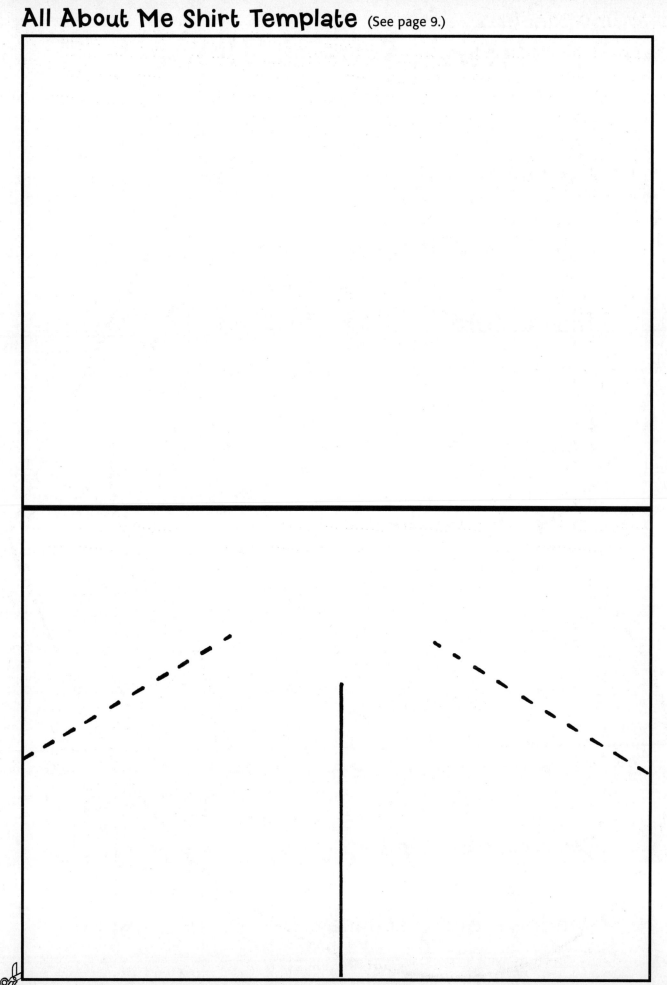

Home, Sweet, Home

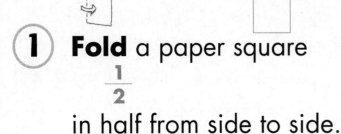 **1** **Fold** a paper square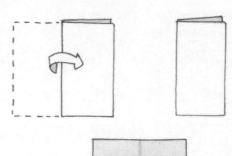

$\frac{1}{2}$

in half from side to side.

Then **unfold**.

 **2** **Fold** in the two top corners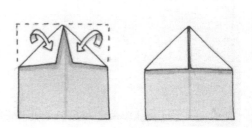

so they meet at the middle.

3 **Fold** back part of one corner. **1**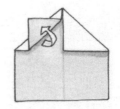

4 **Turn** your paper over.

 **Draw** a roof, a door,

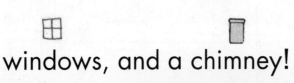 windows, and a chimney!

Valentine Mailer

1 **Write** a note on your heart.

Then **decorate** it.

2 **Turn** your heart

↓

upside down.

Fold in the sides

so they meet at the middle.

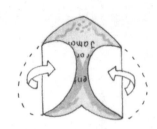

3 **Fold** up the rounded parts

at the bottom.

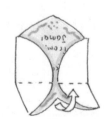

4 **Fold** down the top flap.

Seal with a sticker!

Super Space Shuttle

1 **Fold** a paper square in half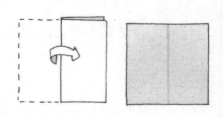

from side to side. Then **unfold**.

2 **Fold** in the two sides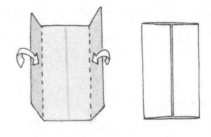

so they meet at the middle.

3 **Fold** in the two top corners.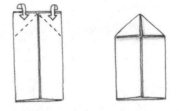

4 **Fold** out the two sides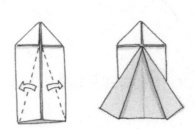

at the bottom.

5 **Turn** the paper over.

Decorate your space shuttle!

Simple Sailboat

1 **Fold** a paper diamond $\frac{1}{2}$ in half from side to side

to make a triangle.

Then **unfold**.

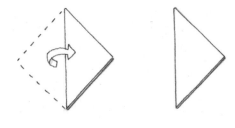

2 **Fold** in the two sides so they

almost meet at the middle.

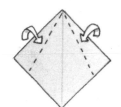

3 **Turn** the paper over.

Fold up part of the bottom corner.

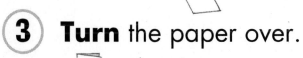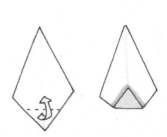

4 **Turn** the paper over again.

Decorate your sailboat!

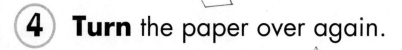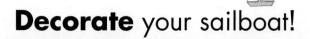

Wintertime Tree

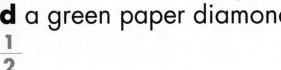

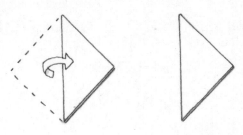

(1) **Fold** a green paper diamond $\frac{1}{2}$ in half from side to side

 to make a triangle.

Then **unfold**.

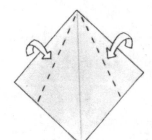 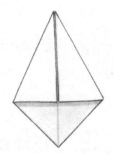

(2) **Fold** in the two sides

so they meet

at the middle.

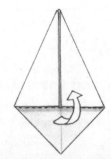 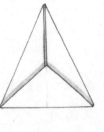

(3) **Fold** up

the bottom corner.

Cut off this bottom strip. Then glue this page to the top of page 23.

22

(4) **Fold** down

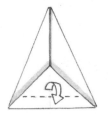 

part of the corner.

(5) **Fold** up the bottom tip.

(6) **Turn** the paper over.

Dab white glitter glue

all over your tree.

Let it snow!

23

All About Me

  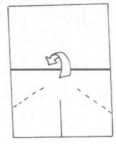 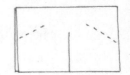

1 **Fold** back the shirt template

____

on the thick black line.

 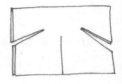

2 **Cut** along

2 - - - - - - -

the two dashed lines.

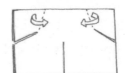 

3 **Fold** down the cut corners

so they meet.

This is the collar.

4 **Draw** your face

on the head template.

 Cut off this bottom strip. Then glue this page to the top of page 25.

24

5 **Glue** on yarn

to make your hair.

6 **Glue** your head

to the shirt

under the collar.

7 **Glue** down the collar.

8 **Color** your shirt.

3

Glue on three buttons!

25

High-Flying Kite

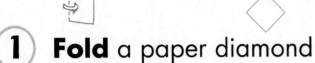

1 **Fold** a paper diamond $\frac{1}{2}$

in half from side to side

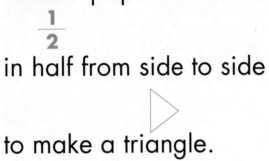

to make a triangle.

Then **unfold**.

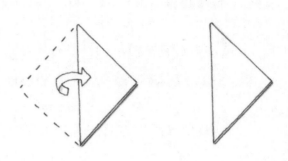

2 **Fold** in the two sides **2**

so they meet at the middle.

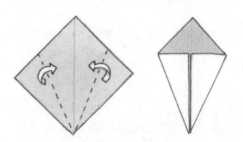

3 **Glue** a piece of yarn

to the bottom.

Let the glue dry.

Cut off this bottom strip. Then glue this page to the top of page 27.

26

(4) Turn the kite over.

Decorate it!

Use crayons, markers, stickers,

and more.

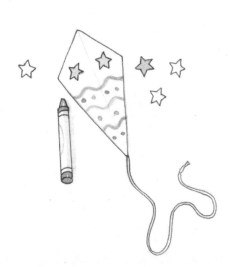

(5) Paint pasta bow ties.

Use different colors.

Let the paint dry.

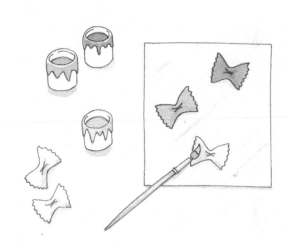

(6) Glue the bow ties

to the tail.

Fly high, pretty kite!

Ice Cream Cone

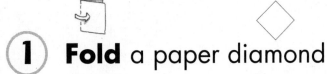 **1** **Fold** a paper diamond $\frac{1}{2}$ in half from side to side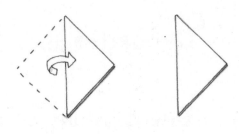

to make a triangle.

 Then **unfold**.

2 **Fold** in the two **2** sides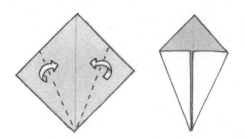

so they meet at the middle.

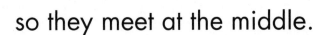

3 **Fold** down the top corner.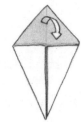

Turn your paper over.

This is the cone.

Cut off this bottom strip. Then glue this page to the top of page 29.

4 What kind of ice cream

will you **make**?

Choose a new paper square.

     4
Fold in all four corners.

5 **Turn** the paper over.

Glue your ice cream

to your cone.

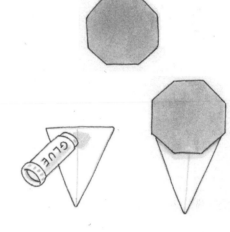

6 **Add** toppings.

Use glitter glue, paper dots,

and more.

Yummy-yummy!

29

Springtime Tulip

1 **Fold** a paper diamond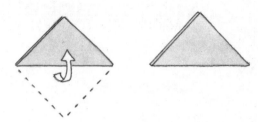

$\frac{1}{2}$

in half from bottom to top

to make a triangle.

2 **Fold** up the two bottom corners.

3 **Take** a green paper diamond.

$\frac{1}{2}$

Fold it in half

from side to side.

Then **unfold**.

4 **Fold** in the two sides

so they meet at the middle.

Cut off this bottom strip. Then glue this page to the top of page 31.

30

(5) **Fold** in the sides again.

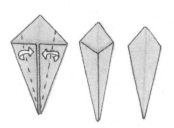

Turn your leaf over.

(6) **Make** another leaf.

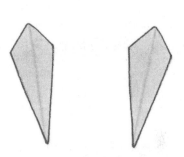

Do steps 3–5 again

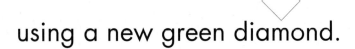

using a new green diamond.

(7) **Glue** your tulip

to a sheet of paper.

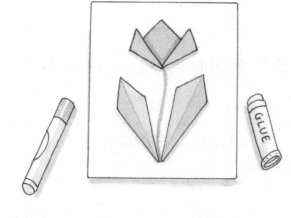

Draw a green stem.

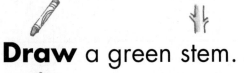

Glue on the leaves.

What a lovely flower!

31

Pretty Picture Frame

1 **Fold** a paper square

$\frac{1}{2}$

in half from side to side.

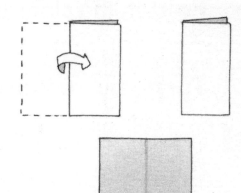

Then **unfold**.

2 **Fold** the square

$\frac{1}{2}$

in half the other way.

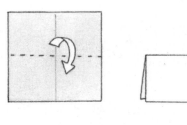

Then **unfold**.

3 **Fold** in all four corners

4

so they meet at the middle.

Now you have a diamond

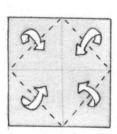

4 △

with four triangles.

Cut off this bottom strip. Then glue this page to the top of page 33.

32

4 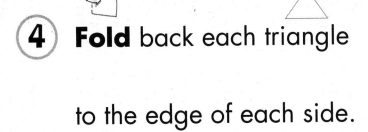 **Fold** back each triangle

to the edge of each side.

5 **Decorate** your frame.

Use crayons, scrap paper,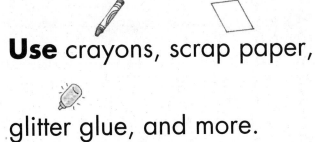

glitter glue, and more.

6 **Glue** a picture

inside your frame.

7 **Glue** down the sides

of your frame.

What a pretty picture frame!

Friendly Fish

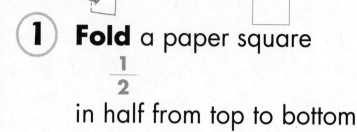 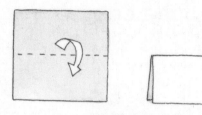

(1) **Fold** a paper square $\frac{1}{2}$

in half from top to bottom

to make a rectangle.

Then **unfold**.

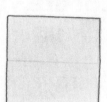

 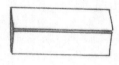

(2) **Fold** in the top

and bottom edges

so they meet at the middle.

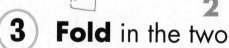

(3) **Fold** in the two **2**

left corners

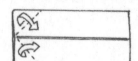

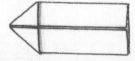

so they meet at the middle.

Cut off this bottom strip. Then glue this page to the top of page 35.

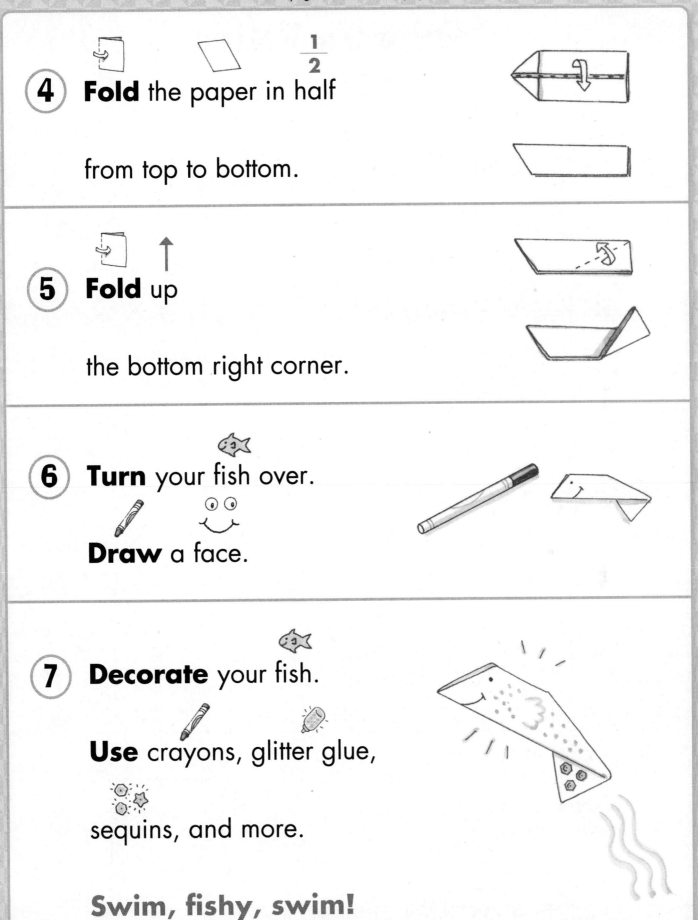

4 **Fold** the paper in half

from top to bottom.

5 **Fold** up

the bottom right corner.

6 **Turn** your fish over.

Draw a face.

7 **Decorate** your fish.

Use crayons, glitter glue,

sequins, and more.

Swim, fishy, swim!

Wonderful Whale

 ① **Fold** a paper diamond

$\dfrac{1}{2}$

in half from top to bottom

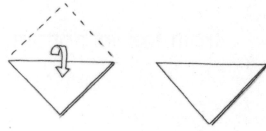

to make a triangle.

 Then **unfold**.

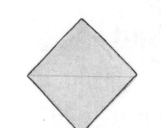

② **Fold** in the top

and bottom corners

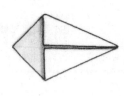

so they meet at the middle.

③ **Fold** in the side corner

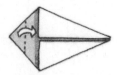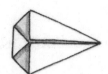

to meet the folded edges.

Cut off this bottom strip. Then glue this page to the top of page 37.

36

4 **Fold** the paper in half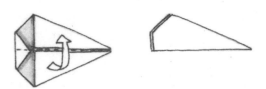

from bottom to top.

5 **Fold** up the thin corner.

This is the whale's tail.

6 **Cut** a slit in the tail.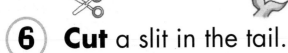

Then **fold** down each side.

7 **Draw** a face.

Glue on a curly ribbon spout.

**Watch your whale
blow its spout!**

Munching Mouse

  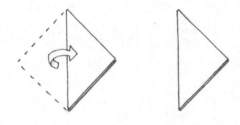

(1) Fold a paper diamond

$\frac{1}{2}$

in half from side to side

to make a triangle.

Then **unfold**.

 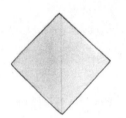

(2) Fold in the two **2** sides

so they meet at the middle.

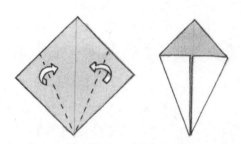

(3) Fold down

the wide top corner.

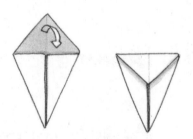

(4) Tuck it under

2

the two sides.

Cut off this bottom strip. Then glue this page to the top of page 39.

38

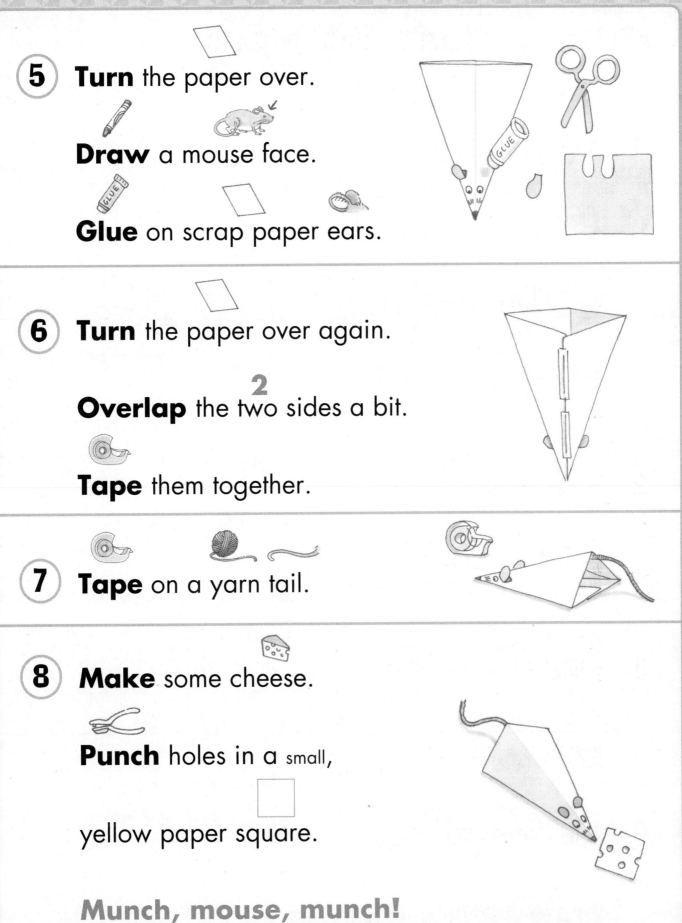

5 **Turn** the paper over.

Draw a mouse face.

Glue on scrap paper ears.

6 **Turn** the paper over again.

2
Overlap the two sides a bit.

Tape them together.

7 **Tape** on a yarn tail.

8 **Make** some cheese.

Punch holes in a small,

yellow paper square.

Munch, mouse, munch!

Cute Kitty Cat

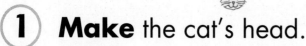

1 **Make** the cat's head.

Fold a paper diamond

$\frac{1}{2}$

in half from bottom to top

to make a triangle.

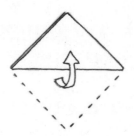

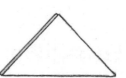

2 **Fold** down the top corner.

3 **Fold** up the two bottom corners.

Turn the paper over.

4 **Glue** on two wiggle eyes.

and a pompom nose.

Draw a smile and whiskers.

Cut off this bottom strip. Then glue this page to the top of page 41.

40

5 **Make** the body.

Fold a new paper square

$\frac{1}{2}$

in half from corner to corner

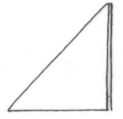

to make a triangle.

6 **Fold** down

the bottom left corner.

7 **Glue** your cat's head

to its body.

Mee-owww!

41

Perky Puppy Dog

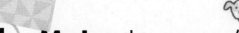

1 **Make** the puppy's head.

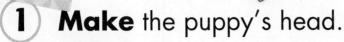

Fold a paper diamond

$\frac{1}{2}$

in half from top to bottom

to make a triangle.

2 **Fold** up the top layer

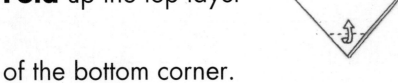

of the bottom corner.

3 **Make** two ears.

Fold down

the top two corners.

4 **Draw** a face.

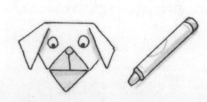

Cut off this bottom strip. Then glue this page to the top of page 43.

42

5 **Glue** on a tongue.

 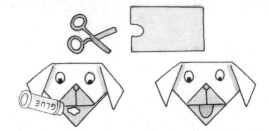

Use pink scrap paper.

6 **Make** the body.

Fold a new paper square

$\frac{1}{2}$

in half from corner to corner

to make a triangle.

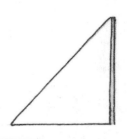

7 **Fold** in

the bottom left corner.

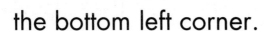 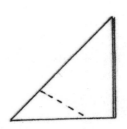 

8 **Glue** your puppy's head

to its body.

Your puppy is ready to play!

Pink Piggy Puppet

1 **Fold** a pink paper diamond

$\frac{1}{2}$

in half from top to bottom

to make a triangle.

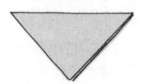

2 **Use** scissors

to round off

the bottom corner.

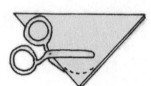

3 **Fold** up

the rounded corner.

This is the snout.

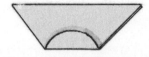

Cut off this bottom strip. Then glue this page to the top of page 45.

(4) Fold down the tips

2

of the top two corners.

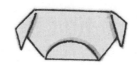

These are the ears.

(5) Glue on two wiggle eyes.

2

Add two stick-on paper circles.

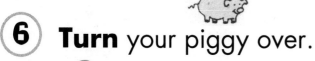

(6) Turn your piggy over.

Tape a craft stick to the back.

Oink-oink! Oink-oink!

Little Red Pecking Hen

(1) **Fold** a red paper diamond

$\frac{1}{2}$

in half from top to bottom

to make a triangle.

Then **unfold**.

---

(2) **Fold** in the top

and bottom corners

 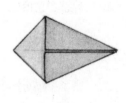

so they meet at the middle.

---

(3) **Turn** the paper over.

 $\frac{1}{2}$

Fold it in half

from top to bottom.

 Cut off this bottom strip. Then glue this page to the top of page 47.

46

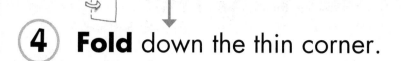

(4) **Fold** down the thin corner.

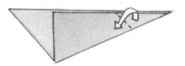

Make a sharp crease.

This is the hen's head.

(5) **Glue** down the head.

(6) **Draw** two eyes.

Glue on craft feathers.

(7) **Help** your hen eat corn.

Gently **press** down on its tail.

Peck, peck, peck!

47

Chatty Cow Puppet

1 **Fold** a paper square 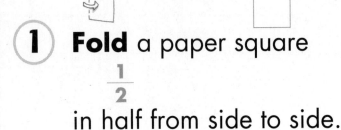 $\frac{1}{2}$

in half from side to side.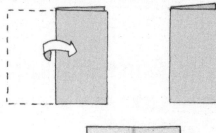

Then **unfold**.

2 **Fold** in the two sides **2**

so they meet at the middle.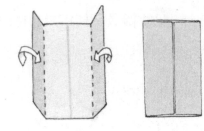

3 **Fold** the paper in half 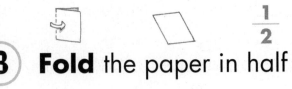 $\frac{1}{2}$

from side to side.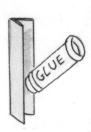

Glue closed.

4 **Fold** the paper in half 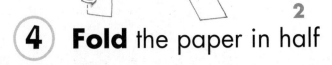 $\frac{1}{2}$

from top to bottom.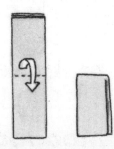

Cut off this bottom strip. Then glue this page to the top of page 49.

(5)  **1** **Fold** back one end.

(6) **Turn** the paper over.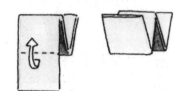

Fold back the other end.

(7) **Draw** two eyes on your cow.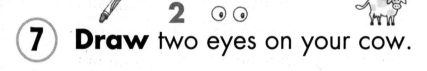

2

Add two stick-on paper circles.

(8) **Make** two ears and a tongue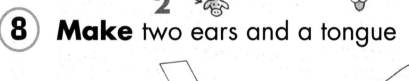

2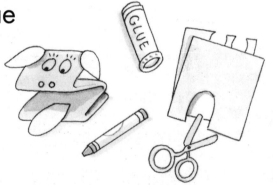

from scrap paper.

Glue them on.

(9) **Use** your hand

to make your cow talk.

Moo!

Mooooo!

Big Red Barn

1 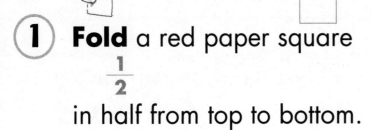   **Fold** a red paper square $\frac{1}{2}$ in half from top to bottom.

2 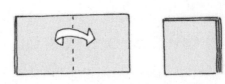 **Fold** the rectangle $\frac{1}{2}$ in half from side to side.

  Then **unfold**.

3 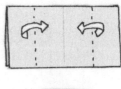 **Fold** in the two sides

so they meet at the middle.

4   **Fold** down

the top inside corners.

 Cut off this bottom strip. Then glue this page to the top of page 51.

50

5  **Unfold** each side.

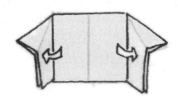

6 **Use** your finger

to open the folded corners.

7 **Press** them flat.

8 **Decorate** your barn.

Draw doors and windows.

Who lives inside

your barn?

Draw pictures!

Slither-and-Slide Snake

1 **Fold** down one small **corner** of a paper diamond.

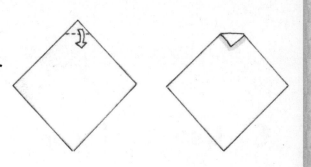

2 **Turn** the paper over.

Make another fold

the same size.

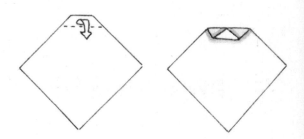

3 **Fold** the rest

of the paper

back and forth

in the same way.

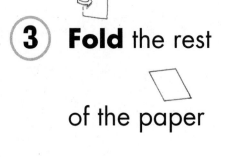
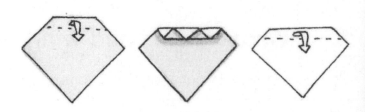
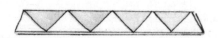

Cut off this bottom strip. Then glue this page to the top of page 53.

4  **Draw** two eyes

1 at one end of your snake.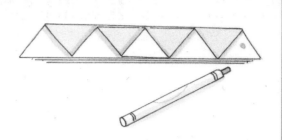

5 **Tape** your snake closed

along the top and bottom.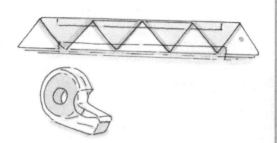

6 **Fold** your snake

back and forth.

7 **Tape** a piece of string

to your snake's head.

**Make your snake
slither and slide!**

53

Fluttering Butterfly

1 **Fold** down one small **corner**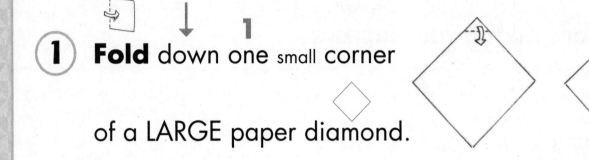

of a LARGE paper diamond.

2 **Turn** the paper over.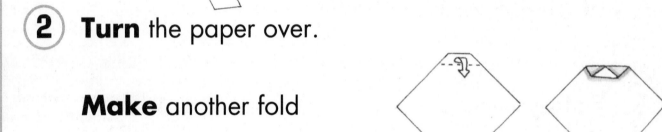

Make another fold

the same size.

3 **Fold** the rest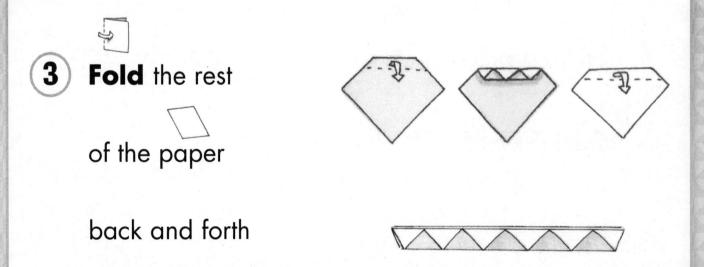

of the paper

back and forth

in the same way.

Cut off this bottom strip. Then glue this page to the top of page 55.

54

4 **Do** steps 1–3 again

using a small **paper diamond.**

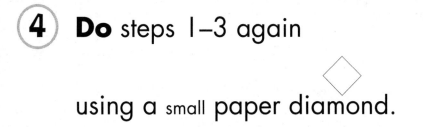

5 **Put** the two sets

of wings together.

6 **Bend** a pipe cleaner in half.

7 **Twist** it around

the middle of the wings.

Curl the ends.

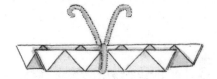

8 **Spread** out the wings.

Flutter, flutter, butterfly!

Penguin Pal

1 **Fold** a white paper diamond $\frac{1}{2}$ in half from side to side.

 Then **unfold.**

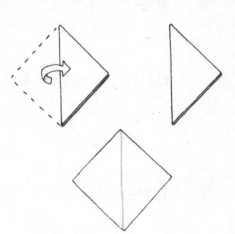

2  **Fold** in the two **2** sides

so they meet at the middle.

3  **Fold** down the thin top corner.

 This is the penguin's head.

4  **Turn** the paper over.

  Fold up the wide

bottom corner.

 Cut off this bottom strip. Then glue this page to the top of page 57.

56

(5) **Fold** back

on the middle crease.

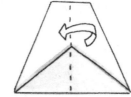

(6) **Pull** up on the beak.

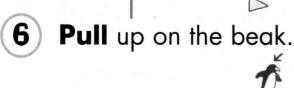

Then **press** the head flat.

(7) **Fold** back the flap

on each side

to make flippers.

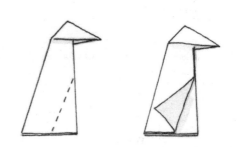

(8) **Color** your penguin.

Draw a face.

Make your penguin walk and waddle!

Big Bird Mask

(1) **Fold** a LARGE paper diamond

$\frac{1}{2}$

in half from side to side

to make a triangle.

Then **unfold**.

(2) **Fold** in the sides

so they meet at the middle.

(3) **Fold** down

the wide top corner.

 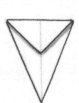

(4) **Fold** up the thin bottom

corner to meet the top edge.

Cut off this bottom strip. Then glue this page to the top of page 59.

58

 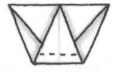

5 **Fold** down part

of the thin corner.

This is the beak.

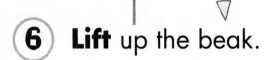

6 **Lift** up the beak.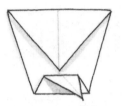

7 **Ask** a grownup

to cut holes for eyes.

8 **Punch** a hole on each side.

 2

Tie on two pieces of string.

9 **Decorate** your mask!

Use crayons, feathers, and more.

Perfect Party Hat

(1) **Fold** a LARGE paper diamond

$\frac{1}{2}$

in half from top to bottom

to make a triangle.

---

(2) **Fold** one top corner

across to meet

the opposite side.

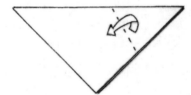 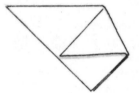

---

(3) **Fold** the other top corner

across to meet

the other side.

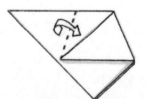

 Cut off this bottom strip. Then glue this page to the top of page 61.

60

4  **Fold** up

1

one of the bottom corners.

 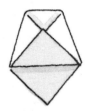

5 **Turn** the hat over.

 Fold up

the other bottom corner.

6 **Decorate** your hat!

Use crayons, yarn, feathers,

scrap paper, and more.

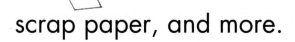

It's party time!

Cool Crown

1  **Fold** a paper diamond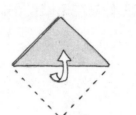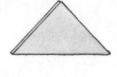

$\frac{1}{2}$

in half from bottom to top

to make a triangle.

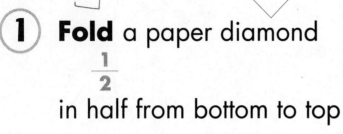

---

2 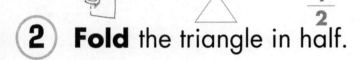 **Fold** the triangle in half.

$\frac{1}{2}$

Then **unfold**.

---

3 **Fold** in the two side corners

2

so they meet at the middle.

Then **unfold**.

---

4 **Do** steps 1–3 again.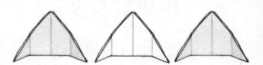

3

Use three more paper diamonds.

 Cut off this bottom strip. Then glue this page to the top of page 63.

62

5 **Slip** each folded corner

into another corner.

↑

Line up the folds.

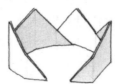

6 **Tape** around the inside

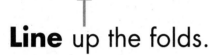

to hold the crown together.

7 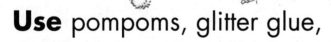 **Decorate** your crown!

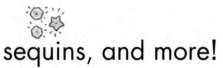 **Use** pompoms, glitter glue,

sequins, and more!

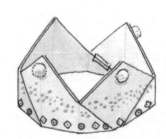

**Wear your crown!
Are you a king
or a queen?**

Origami Square Template